Creeds
in the
Bible

FREDERICK W. DANKER

Concordia Publishing House

St. Louis, Mo.

Concordia Publishing House, St. Louis, Missouri
Concordia Publishing House Ltd., London, E. C. 1
© 1966 Concordia Publishing House

Library of Congress Catalog Card No. 66-29454

MANUFACTURED IN THE UNITED STATES OF AMERICA

Biblical Monographs ❋ ❋

Concordia Biblical Monographs are designed to acquaint readers with current developments in Biblical interpretation. Some of the authors merely report positions of Biblical scholars on specific issues without evaluating them. Others present a constructive essay on a subject of Biblical theology.

In CREEDS IN THE BIBLE Frederick W. Danker discusses creedal confessions in Old and New Testament to increase appreciation for Biblical expressions of faith and the historic creeds of the church.

Contents

Preface

"Life, liberty, and the pursuit of happiness." This is the slogan in the preamble to the Constitution of the United States of America. For some it is a political and a social creed to be taken seriously. Others, like a certain voluble senator in one of the light operas, are too busy defending the Constitution to take the time to read it. As a result our country is riddled with legal inequities and social injustices. Similarly, the creeds of Christendom are recited in multitudinous chorus with monotonous fidelity, but only here and there can it be said that "the Church is on the boil," as an English vicar expressed it.

One way to increase the heat is to study afresh the Biblical expressions of faith. What did the early Christian mean when he said, "I believe that Jesus is Christ and Lord"? And how did he understand his convictions in relation to those of his spiritual ancestors, the Israelites of the Old Testament?

7

This little book therefore does not enter into the intricacies of dogmatical debates but is designed for the reader who would identify more intimately with men and women for whom faith was more than a status symbol in a steepled club. It does not engage in antiquarian inquiry but tries to lay its finger on the pulse of people for whom confession of faith was often an occupational hazard. Unless otherwise noted, all citations of the Scriptures are from the Revised Standard Version, 1959 revision. Stylistic alterations of this version are the responsibility of the editor of this series.

Saint Mark the Evangelist
April 25, 1966

Confessions of Faith

"I will give thanks to the Lord with my whole heart; I will tell of all Thy wonderful deeds" (Ps. 9:1). What is striking in this statement is the close relationship between the impact of God's action on the individual and his corresponding articulation of the experience. Recognition of God's mercy leads to a worshipful verbalization of specific aspects of God's action. Such a common confession of faith is to all practical intent a creedal expression of the community.

One of the basic confessions of the Old Testament is expressed in Deut. 26:5-10:

> A wandering Aramean was my father; and he went down into Egypt and sojourned there, few in number; and there he became a nation, great, mighty, and populous. And the Egyptians treated us harshly and afflicted us and laid upon us hard bondage. Then

9

we cried to the Lord, the God of our fathers, and the Lord heard our voice and saw our affliction, our toil, and our oppression; and the Lord brought us out of Egypt with a mighty hand and an outstretched arm, with great terror, with signs and wonders; and He brought us into this place and gave us this land, a land flowing with milk and honey. And behold, now I bring the first of the fruit of the ground, which Thou, O Lord, hast given me.

The rubric for this creed is: "You shall make response before the Lord your God." (V. 5)

The approach in the New Testament is similar, only here the focus is on Jesus Christ as the culmination of God's redemptive action in behalf of Israel. Jesus Himself makes a good confession before Pontius Pilate, according to 1 Tim. 6:13. Because of His uncompromising dedication to His task and total commitment to His Father's purpose He is called in Rev. 1:5 "the faithful Witness" and in Rev. 3:14 "the faithful and true Witness." In contrast to Peter, who concluded his denials of his Lord with the words: "I do not know this Man of whom you speak" (Mark 14:71), Jesus affirms His Messianic mission before the high priest (" 'Are you the Christ, the Son of the Blessed?' And Jesus said, 'I am; and you will see the Son of Man sitting at the right hand of Power and coming with the clouds of heaven,' " Mark 14: 61-62) and before Pilate ("And Pilate asked Him, 'Are you the King of the Jews?' And He answered him, 'You have said so,' " 15:2).

Confessing Jesus is not an insignificant matter.

According to Rom. 10:9-10, "If you confess with your lips that Jesus is Lord and believe in your heart that God raised Him from the dead, you will be saved. For man believes with his heart and so is justified, and he confesses with his lips and so is saved."

The vapid sentiment, "It doesn't matter what you believe," would have sounded strange to members of the early Christian community. When men encountered Jesus, they could not escape the realization that in *this* Person they had come to a crossroads. Theologians did not know what to do with Him. "If we let Him go on thus, everyone will believe in Him, and the Romans will come and destroy both our holy place and our nation" (John 11:48). "Do you think that I have come to give peace on earth?" asked Jesus. "No, I tell you, but rather division" (Luke 12:51). "Follow Me," directed Jesus at a tax collector's office (Luke 5:27). "Who do men say that I am?" was followed up by: "But who do *you* say that I am?" (Mark 8:27, 29). And over two early Christians named Hymenaeus and Alexander we read this epitaph: They "made shipwreck of their faith." (1 Tim. 1:19)

The Western text of Acts 8:37 attests the solemnity with which the Christians very early in the history of their community must have approached their baptism and thereby acceptance of their responsibilities as members of the redeemed community. According to this ancient reading Philip said in reply to the eunuch's question whether there was anything to prevent his baptism, "'If you believe with all your heart, you may.' And he replied, 'I believe that Jesus Christ is the Son of God.'" The responses undoubtedly varied, but there could be no mistaking the focal point of the fresh turn the believer's life had taken. Thus the centurion "rejoiced with all his household that he had believed in God" (Acts 16:34). In the gatherings of his family in the faith opportunity would be found to affirm significant actions of this one Lord and Savior, which would also make their way into the catechetical instruction. In such balanced phrases as "put to death in the flesh but made alive in the spirit" (1 Peter 3:18) we may hear a repeated confessional note. In his approach to the problem of the resurrection Paul says, "I delivered to you as of first importance what I also received, that Christ died for our sins in accordance with the Scriptures, that He was buried, that He was raised on the third day in accordance with the Scriptures." (1 Cor. 15:3-4)

By utilizing established creedal affirmations as his indicative base, the apostle is able to move forward in his favorite manner to the imperative: the practical concern. He argues in the subsequent verses (12-19) that if the Corinthians claim that the dead are not raised then their creedal affirmation concerning the resurrection of Jesus is also invalid. A similar approach appears to underlie the thoughts expressed in Phil. 2:6-11, which may well be, at least in part, an early Christological hymn:

> [Christ Jesus] though He was in the form of God, did not count equality with God a thing to be grasped but emptied Himself, taking the form of a servant, being born in the likeness of men. And being found in human form He humbled Himself and became obedient unto death, even death on a cross. Therefore God has highly exalted Him and bestowed on Him the name which is above every name, that at the name of Jesus every knee should bow, in heaven and on earth and under the earth, and every tongue confess that Jesus Christ is Lord, to the glory of God the Father.

That their Lord neither gave grudgingly nor expected sparingly was well known in the early Christian community. He did not go up to come down: "If any man would come after Me, let him deny himself and take up his cross daily and follow Me. For whoever would save his life will lose it; and whoever loses his life for My sake, he will save it." (Luke 9:23-24)

That was His price and it has never fluctuated. In the face of social and political persecution creedal statements identifying Jesus as the Christ and as Lord were the necessary response of Christians who realized the necessity of taking sides openly and accepting the risk of identification with One whose absolute claims are not popular with the world. As Tertullian put it: "We are not worried by these persecutions, for we have joined this church fully accepting the terms of the agreement with us as men whose very souls are not our own." For Christians in such situations the word confession spelled admission of guilt, and there was no pleading the Fifth Amendment.

A consistent accent on Jesus Christ lent unity to the greatly varied creedal expression found in the New Testament. The rich diversity of gifts and early untrammeled functioning of the Holy Spirit were not compatible with uniform structures. From the diverse character of such passages as 1 Cor. 15: 3-6; Eph. 4:4-6; Phil. 2:6-11; and 1 Tim. 3:16 it is clear that the joint recitation throughout the early church of something like an Apostles' Creed is unknown. And even in the case of the statements made in the passages mentioned we cannot be sure where the apostle's adaptation begins and the formal affirmation of some segment or segments of the church ends. The same Spirit who was operative in the Christian communities in their worship and their varied ministry was creatively active in the writers of the New Testament, and their documents became the standard against which confessions of the faith were to be measured. Out of diversity emerged uniformity as the mushrooming of heresy led to more precise formulations.

Early stages of the reaction to false teaching are extant in the First Epistle of John. "Who is the liar but he who denies that Jesus is the Christ?" (1 John 2:22). And on the affirmative side: "Every spirit which confesses that Jesus Christ has come in the flesh is of God, and every spirit which does not confess Jesus is not of God" (1 John 4:2-3). But God's action in Jesus the Christ is always the main concern, and neither the Nicene nor the Athanasian Creed, despite their more philosophical terminology, shifts appreciably from Peter's confession in Matt. 16:16: "You are the Christ, the Son of the living God."

As we observed at the beginning of this chapter, a common confession of faith may be called a creedal expression. But we also noted that the early Christian communities had no single uniform creedal formulation. However, they did express themselves in ways which clearly accent their thinking about the central Figure in their cultus. In the chapters that follow we have tried to be sensitive to the mind of the early Christian communities, especially in their self-understanding as the spiritual heirs of the Israelites of the Old Testament era. Instead of isolating and analyzing specific passages containing what may or may not be communal creedal statements, we are confining ourselves to the principal summary affirmations that have reference to Jesus especially as He is understood in relation to the Old Testament. In view of this objective we shall take occasion to ponder the significance of such basic affirmations and understandings as are to be found in Old Testament passages like Ex. 19:3-6; 20:2; Deut. 6:4; 26:5-10; Is. 52:7-10; Jer. 31:31-34; Hos. 4:1-6.

2

One God

"Hear, O Israel: The Lord our God is one Lord" (Deut. 6:4). In these words, called the Shema, the hard core of the ancient faith of Israel finds expression. The dramatic date of their utterance is the occasion of Moses' farewell to his people before their entrance into the land of Canaan. Behind them lies a great series of deliverances, before them the gifts of promise. Jahweh is the sole source of both, and therefore Israel is reminded that she belongs without reservation to Him: "This day you have become the people of the Lord your God" (Deut. 27:9). In Josiah's time this exhortation found literary expression and marked the climax of the demand to exterminate everything that conflicted with the worship of Jahweh as the only God.

In contrast to the modern question: "Is there a

god?" the Israelite asked, "Who is He?" And the answer is: He is unique, and there is none to share His name. God is not the object of man's search. No amount of religious genius can comprehend this One. God investigates man, man does not investigate God. God creates man and defines his proper sphere and role. When Adam's attempts to become like God fail, his Creator goes out to find him. In the cool of the evening He calls out to him, "Where are you?" Man hides, but God searches the depths of his being. God is not the product of man's research.

Above the circle of the earth He sits (Is. 40:22). And when man thinks he is accomplishing great things, God shows His contempt for his puny efforts, for to save His eyes, He comes down to get a closer view of all the commotion at Babel (Gen. 11:7). "He who sits in the heavens laughs; the Lord has them in derision." (Ps. 2:4)

The God of Israel is indeed one who keeps hidden (Is. 45:15), and His hiddenness is reflected in the Old Testament prohibition of images. Israel's God cannot be displayed in any earthly form (Ex. 20:4). He is the Creator and is responsible for all earthly forms and for the natural processes. Hence, along with the unquestioning affirmation of God's existence in Gen. 1:1, we see accented His unique and exclusive position. He is the One who made the stars, and He is responsible for the week with its seven days. No deities can compete with Him.

Whatever astral forces may be imagined by man, God is supreme. Idols are silver and gold; our God is in the heavens (Ps. 115:3, 4; cf. Ps. 135). If He appears to man, it is in dreams (Gen. 28:12-15), or He permits Moses to see His back. (Ex. 33:23)

The Lord who has made the heavens and the earth is the Creator also of Israel. Unlike the nations around her, who engage in fertility cults, Israel worships a God who is not observed through the rhythm of nature but through an intervention in Israel's own history. God reached down into history and by a mighty act of deliverance made Abraham's descendants through Isaac a mighty nation. The preamble to the Decalog reads: "I am the Lord your God, who brought you out of the land of Egypt, out of the house of bondage" (Ex. 20:2). The Exodus is God's great act which is never to be forgotten. For all time to come Israel is to remember — on that night we were delivered. This act of intervention in her history was but the beginning of further demonstrations of God's concern for His people. The feats of the judges, miraculous deliverances from the enemy, release from captivity — all this becomes a part of Israel's commentary on the uniqueness of her God.

Israel was not chosen because she was mighty and powerful. On the contrary, she was the least of the nations. But God chose her, elected her. This understanding about herself is the key to her relationship with God. God elects her to a covenant relationship. This covenant He makes is not a compact between equals. God offers the covenant. In this suzerainty compact God promises to take care of Israel. He accepts responsibility for her.

> "Say therefore to the people of Israel, 'I am the Lord, and I will bring you out from under the burdens of the Egyptians, and I will deliver you from their bondage, and I will redeem you with an outstretched arm and with great acts of judgment, and I will take you for My people, and I will be your God; and you shall know that I am the Lord your God, who has brought you out from under the burdens of the Egyptians.'" (Ex. 6:6-8)

Israel, on the other hand, must accept the mandates of her Lord, for He is the One who brought Israel out of Egypt:

> And Moses went up to God, and the Lord called him out of the mountain, saying, "Thus you shall say to the house of Jacob and tell the people of Israel: You have seen what I did to the Egyptians and how I bore you on eagles' wings and brought you to Myself. Now therefore, if you will obey My voice and keep My covenant, you shall be My own possession among all peoples; for all the earth is Mine, and you shall be to Me a kingdom of priests and a holy nation. These are the words which you shall speak to the Children of Israel." (Ex. 19:3-6)

The Israelites are to have unwavering trust in Jahweh. He will do His part as their suzerain Lord. He will "bless" their bread and water, and "will take sickness away" from their midst (Ex. 23:25). He will drive out their enemies before them (vv. 22, 29) and "deliver the inhabitants of the land" into their hand

(v. 31). In the Ten Commandments we have the rights of the suzerain specified. "Thou shalt not" defines the limitations within which Israel as a vassal to the Lord may function. Israel belongs to the Lord, not the Lord to Israel. The kings of the time tolerated no grumbling from their vassals, and any murmuring against God would be a violation of Israel's obligation. Hence at Kibroth-hattaavah "the anger of the Lord was kindled against the people, and the Lord smote the people with a very great plague." (Num. 11:33)

A strong ethical note runs through almost all of the Old Testament. God knows Israel, and Israel shows that she understands her relationship to God through obedience to His mandates. A mysterious passage in 1 Peter 1:1-2 explains well the situation. We are taken back to the event at Sinai. Israel is sprinkled by the blood, and she promises to observe all the things written in the book of the Law. Likewise the readers of 1 Peter are reminded that they have been sprinkled with the blood of Jesus Christ for obedience. The Law of God, in brief, does not bring moral obligations into being. The Law rather affirms these obligations. Hence the words of Ex. 20:2 ("I am the Lord your God, who brought you out of the land of Egypt, out of the house of bondage") are the prelude to the statement of the covenant obligations.

God knows Israel. The question is: Will Israel know God? Israel may think that she can treat God as one hoodwinks an unwary buyer. Then she will fall into hypocrisy and formalism. These are the glaucoma of a nation that fools itself that it sees when it does not see. Israel failed to heed the voices of her prophets, and she insisted on breaking the covenant God had made with her. Hos. 4:1-6 well describes her plight:

> Hear the word of the Lord, O people of Israel; for the Lord has a controversy with the inhabitants of the land. There is no faithfulness or kindness and no knowledge of God in the land; there is swearing, lying, killing, stealing, and committing adultery; they break all bounds and murder follows murder. Therefore the land mourns, and all who dwell in it languish, and also the beasts of the field and the birds of the air; and even the fish of the sea are taken away. Yet let no one contend, and let none accuse, for with you is My contention, O priest. You shall stumble by day, the prophet also shall stumble with you by night; and I will destroy your mother. My people are destroyed for lack of knowledge; because you have rejected knowledge, I reject you from being a priest to Me. And since you have forgotten the Law of your God, I also will forget your children.

Righteousness makes for understanding, but the more His people sin, the more God is hidden from their eyes. (Is. 6:9)

The warnings accompanying the first covenant were unmistakable. The long prophecy of woe in Deut. 28, which echoes Lev. 26, concludes on a dreadfully ironic note: "And the Lord will bring

21

you back in ships to Egypt, a journey which I promised that you should never make again; and there you shall offer yourselves for sale to your enemies as male and female slaves, but no man will buy you" (Deut. 28:68). Yet God is faithful, and antedating the covenant with Israel is His covenant with Abraham:

> Behold, My covenant is with you, and you shall be the father of a multitude of nations. No longer shall your name be Abram, but your name shall be Abraham; for I have made you the father of a multitude of nations. I will make you exceedingly fruitful; and I will make nations of you, and kings shall come forth from you. And I will establish My covenant between Me and you and your descendants after you throughout their generations for an everlasting covenant, to be God to you and to your descendants after you. And I will give to you and to your descendants after you the land of your sojournings, all the land of Canaan, for an everlasting possession; and I will be their God. (Gen. 17:4-8)

In order to keep His covenant with Abraham, God has no choice in view of Israel's broken troth but to make a new covenant. As the Lord says to Jeremiah: "If I have not established My covenant with day and night and the ordinances of heaven and earth, then I will reject the descendants of Jacob and David My servant and will not choose one of his descendants to rule over the seed of Abraham, Isaac, and Jacob. For I will restore their fortunes and will have mercy upon them" (33:25-26). The

hope of that covenant is described earlier in Jer.
31:31-34 (cf. Hos. 2:14-23):

> Behold, the days are coming, says the Lord, when
> I will make a new covenant with the house of Israel
> and the house of Judah, not like the covenant which
> I made with their fathers when I took them by the
> hand to bring them out of the land of Egypt, My
> covenant which they broke, though I was their Hus-
> band, says the Lord. But this is the covenant which
> I will make with the house of Israel after those days,
> says the Lord: I will put My Law within them, and I
> will write it upon their hearts; and I will be their
> God, and they shall be My people. And no longer
> shall each man teach his neighbor and each his
> brother, saying, "Know the Lord," for they shall
> all know Me, from the least of them to the greatest,
> says the Lord; for I will forgive their iniquity, and
> I will remember their sin no more.

On the night that Jesus was betrayed that new
covenant became a reality. Jesus executed another
mighty act, the act of giving Himself in a showdown
battle with Satan. On the night of His betrayal the
Israel of the new covenant took shape. The Shema
is still valid: "Hear, O Israel: The Lord our God is
one Lord." The covenant He made with mankind in
Jesus is in continuity with His action of old (cf.
Gal. 3).

As Israel of old had a mission to the world
(Is. 42:7; Jer. 33:9), so Israel of the new covenant
has her mission. St. Paul endorses the words of
Isaiah:

> How beautiful upon the mountains are the feet of

him who brings good tidings, who publishes peace, who brings good tidings of good, who publishes salvation, who says to Zion, "Your God reigns." Hark, your watchmen lift up their voice, together they sing for joy; for eye to eye they see the return of the Lord to Zion. Break forth together into singing, you waste places of Jerusalem; for the Lord has comforted His people, He has redeemed Jerusalem. The Lord has bared His holy arm before the eyes of all the nations; and all the ends of the earth shall see the salvation of our God. (Is. 52:7-19; cf. Rom. 10:15)

Since God is one, all mankind is included in the mission objective. To say the Shema with ancient Israel means to repeat the divine intent: God "desires all men to be saved and to come to the knowledge of the truth" (1 Tim. 2:4). God is no longer hidden, for as Dietrich Bonhoeffer beautifully says, the church is "founded in the revelation of God's heart." The outstanding commentary on all this is Eph. 4:4-6, which may well contain phraseology from an early creed: "There is one body and one Spirit, just as you were called to the one hope that belongs to your call, one Lord, one faith, one Baptism, one God and Father of us all, who is above all and through all and in all."

3

Jesus Is the Christ

Into the life of gods shall he come;
    gods mingled with heroes
Shall he behold, and the gods themselves
    shall gladly behold him,

. . . .

Ruling a world at peace thro' the noble acts
    of his father.
Even thy cradle, O Babe, shall pour
    forth flow'rs to caress thee,
Snakes shall perish, and plants whose fruit
    is treacherous poison.*

These words from the pen of Rome's epic poet
utter some of the yearning which found expression
in the complex messianic thinking of the world into

* As translated by Thomas Fletcher Royds in his *Virgil and
Isaiah: A Study of the Pollio* (Oxford, 1918), p. 77.

which Jesus Christ was born. So varied and blurred was the popular picture that on one occasion Jesus asked, "Who do the people say that I am?" And they answered, "John the Baptist; but others say Elijah; and others that one of the old prophets has arisen." And He said to them, "But who do you say that I am?" And Peter answered, "The Christ of God" (Luke 9:18-20). In other words, there was no single blueprint followed by Jesus' contemporaries. Roughly speaking, there are three strains of Messianic hope: political, apocalyptic, and moral.

POLITICAL EXPECTATION

The word Messiah means "anointed," and in Israel it was the king who was regularly viewed as the anointed one. Between the king and Israel's God there was a close relationship. Since the king is the Lord's anointed, his person is sacred. Therefore David refuses to lay a hand on Saul (1 Sam. 24). In view of the inviolability of the king's person, not to speak of the Messiah's office, the words in Luke 9:22 were met with incredulity by the disciples: "The Son of Man must suffer many things and be rejected by the elders and chief priests and scribes and be killed and on the third day be raised." Suffering *or* death was anticipated in connection with some popular thinking about the Messiah, but not both.

The king is also endowed with the Spirit of God. According to 1 Sam. 16:13, "the Spirit of the

Lord came mightily upon David from that day forward." Significantly St. Luke captures this accent in connection with Jesus. His conception is through the power of the Spirit (1:35). John, associated with him in the infancy narratives, is to be "filled with the Holy Spirit" (1:15). Simeon is alerted to His arrival through the Holy Spirit (2:26). At His baptism the Holy Spirit "descended upon Him in bodily form, as a dove, and a voice came from heaven: 'Thou art My beloved Son; with Thee I am well pleased'" (3:22). He is led by the Spirit into the wilderness to be tempted by the devil (4:1-2). By the finger of God, that is, by the Spirit of God, he casts out demons (11:20). In the Book of Acts the work of Jesus is documented as authentically Messianic by the receipt of the Spirit on all sides.

The description of David's dynasty in 2 Sam. 7 made a deep impression on Israel, and the concluding words were to be underscored heavily in the apostolic church: "And your house and your kingdom shall be made sure forever before Me; your throne shall be established forever" (v. 16). When Israel came under foreign domination, her mind naturally reflected on the past glory, and her hopes were fanned by the patterned phrases which exalted the Davidic reign. According to Psalm of Solomon 17, a pseudepigraphical work from the period before A. D. 70, the conquered heathen will come and restore the scattered of Israel when the Messiah makes His appearance. When Jesus proclaimed the "ac-

ceptable year of the Lord" in Nazareth (Luke 4:19),
all eyes were focused on Him. And when He said,
" 'Today this scripture has been fulfilled in your
hearing,' . . . all spoke well of Him and wondered
at the gracious words which proceeded out of His
mouth" (4:22). The good news to the poor seemed
to offer deliverance for anxious Israel. But nothing
happened. Instead He said, "there were many lepers
in Israel in the time of the prophet Elisha; and none
of them was cleansed but only Naaman the Syrian"
(4:27). Likewise Elijah was sent to only one widow
— and she was in the land of Sidon (v. 26). That was
too much for the people of Nazareth. The potential
candidate for Israel's highest office had let them
down, and they tried to lynch Him on the spot.

Time and again the people tried to make Him a
king, but Jesus resisted these attempts. On one
occasion He addressed the sponsors of this politically
dominated Messianic hope with the question, "How
can they say that the Christ is David's Son?" (20:41).
Some interpreters suggest that Jesus disclaims any
association with the view that the Messiah is David's
Son. But this is not the point of the passage. Accent
is on the how. The religious leaders emphasized the
political dimension. Jesus challenges this limited
interpretation.

There is, in fact, repeated emphasis that Jesus
is David's Son. The emphasis is necessary because
the Messianic affirmation is unthinkable without the
category of Davidic sonship. Thus Joseph is of the

house of David (1:27). The angel announces to Mary that the "Lord God will give to Him the throne of His father David" (1:32). Zechariah says that God "has raised up a horn of salvation for us in the house of His servant David" (1:69). It is in David's city, Bethlehem, that the Child, "who is Christ the Lord," is born. (2:11)

Jesus is David's Son but in His own way!

MORAL EXPECTATION

A second strain in the Messianic expectation is the moral accent. Psalm of Solomon 17 expresses it this way:

> And he shall gather together a holy people, whom he shall lead in righteousness. . . . And he shall not suffer unrighteousness to lodge anymore in their midst, Nor shall there dwell with them any man that knoweth wickedness, For he shall know them, that they are all sons of their God. . . . For all shall be holy and their king the anointed of the Lord. (vv. 28-30, 36) †

The Pharisees were the chief exponents of this moral concern. They were consecrated laymen dedicated to the preservation of the Torah. In obedience to the Torah they saw the possibility of Israel's survival. Their own observance of the Law was meticulous, extending even to the purification of their furniture (Mark 7:3). Segregation of society into

† Translation from R. H. Charles, *The Apocrypha and Pseudepigrapha of the Old Testament in English* (Oxford: Clarendon Press, 1913, 1963), Vol. II, *The Pseudepigrapha*, pp. 649—50.

lawkeepers and lawbreakers was inevitable. It is not surprising therefore that they would find Jesus' attitudes and actions perplexing. Their most common complaint was: "He eats with publicans and sinners." Jesus insisted that He had an intimate relationship with the Father. According to the position of the Pharisees, such an intimate relationship could be maintained only by observing ritual rules and meeting God's ethical expectations. By associating with publicans and sinners Jesus was stating publicly that it was possible to relate to God even without meeting the demands for ritual purity. Such a position was too radical for the Pharisees, and they felt it represented poor judgment on Jesus' part. Hence their opposition.

What they failed to realize was that Jesus had not come to congratulate the righteous but to save the lost (Luke 5:32; cf. 19:10). He tried to explain to them that it was possible to guard God's prerogatives without rejecting the sinner. At the same time He was not in the habit of relying entirely on nondirective counseling relationships, nor did He encourage anyone to blame his moral status on environment or poor housing. To the self-confident young ruler He said, "Sell all that you have and distribute to the poor, and you will have treasure in heaven; and come, follow Me" (Luke 18:22). To the disciples He said, "You cannot serve God and mammon" (Luke 16:13), and, "You . . . must be perfect, as your heavenly Father is perfect." (Matt. 5:48)

St. Paul's experience with the guardians of legal precision ran in similar channels. His pronouncements on freedom from the Law inspired suspicions about the soundness of the apostle's theology. And there is no question that he sponsored what must have seemed to his Jewish colleagues a radical approach to the ethical question. Yet it was this same apostle who asked the question: "What shall we say then? Are we to continue in sin that grace may abound? By no means! How can we who died to sin still live in it?" (Rom. 6:1-2)

APOCALYPTIC

A third major strand in the popular Messianic consciousness was the apocalyptic note. Apocalyptic is the language of national consolation. It sprang up in Israel when her national fortunes were at low ebb. Whereas the Pharisees saw hope for Israel in a moral resurgence, the apocalyptist looked for a cutting of the knot through direct intervention by God. Any prospect for an improvement of the lot of God's people within history is illusory. This age is under the domination of Satan. The new age will be run by God, and Satan will be overthrown. This new age is to be preceded by signs. There would be portents in the heavens (Ezek. 38; 39; Zech. 14: 1-3; Joel 2:30; 3:15-16) and distress in the earth (Joel 3:11-14).

Evidently John the Baptist anticipated the windup of history with the appearing of Jesus. "The axe is laid to the root of the trees," he warned (Luke 3:9). But later on in prison he asked, "Are You He who is to come, or shall we look for another?" (7:19). Jesus did not satisfy the expectation for an end-time fireworks. Instead we find the Gospels affirming that He is the Christ, and yet He speaks of history continuing beyond His earthly life until the time when the Son of Man returns. Some of the portents are reserved for that arrival. As Christians today we find ourselves in a position similar to that of the contemporaries of Jesus. Like them we look for the Messiah. The difference is that we believe He has come once and will return in judgment.

But the New Testament description of the second coming does not satisfy the orthodox apocalyptist. Matt. 25:31-46 indeed displays the Messiah as the King of the nations, but there is no accent on the supremacy of the faithful in Israel. Rather, *all* nations are gathered before the Son of Man, and they are all separated into two groups, those on the right and those on the left. There is no advantage for Israel. And the words spoken by Jesus are reminiscent of Isaiah 58, which declares the attitudes and actions that are desired by Jahweh. Formalism and hypocrisy — these are the moral deadweight in Israel.

To believe in Jesus as the Christ, then, means to endure God's scrutiny of all our own yardsticks whereby we attempt to legitimatize His plans and purposes. It means to accept Jesus as the One in whom God has concentrated His saving purpose. It means to renounce all human standards and criteria and unqualifiedly make this response to God's revelation of Himself in Jesus of Nazareth: This Jesus is the Christ. The form of the creedal statement might fluctuate. Even the confession at Caesarea Philippi is variously rendered "the Christ of God" (Luke 9:20), "the Christ, the Son of the living God" (Matt. 16:16), and simply "the Christ" (Mark 8:29). The appropriateness of the confession in a polemical context can be concluded from the record of Peter's confession before the audience on Pentecost: "Know assuredly that God has made Him both Lord and Christ" (Acts 2:36). The confession is a dominant topic in Paul's witness to his countrymen. Thus he "confounded the Jews who lived in Damascus by proving that Jesus was the Christ" (9:22); in a synagog at Thessalonica he affirmed, "This Jesus, whom I proclaim to you, is the Christ" (17:3); and in Corinth he testified that "the Christ was Jesus" (18:5). It is possible that the dominical word in Matt. 10:32-33 is to be understood as encouragement to make such an overt identification:

> So everyone who acknowledges Me before men I also will acknowledge before My Father who is in heaven; but whoever denies Me before men, I also will deny before My Father who is in heaven.

In any event the record of Jesus' own self-attestation as the Christ in answer to the high priest's question: "Are you the Christ, the Son of the Blessed?" (Mark 14:61) and its juxtaposition to Peter's denials could leave no doubt in anyone's mind that there was no room for hesitation on this score. Certainly 1 John 2:22 ("Who is the liar but he who denies that Jesus is the Christ?") calls for an unequivocal statement of belief in the face of docetism. And John 9:22 ("His parents said this because they feared the Jews, for the Jews had already agreed that if anyone should confess Him to be Christ, he was to be put out of the synagog") suggests that excommunication was a not infrequent consequence of confession of Jesus as the Christ. The extent to which this formula pervades the canonical writings suggests that it may well be the earliest confession.

4

Jesus Is the Son of God

In her response to Jesus' direct question at the funeral of Lazarus, Martha confesses, "Yes, Lord; I believe that You are the Christ, the Son of God" (John 11:27). Similarly Nathanael answers, "Rabbi, You are the Son of God" (John 1:49). According to Matt. 16:16, Peter replies to Jesus' inquiry, "You are the Christ, the Son of the living God." We have already had occasion to refer to the curious reading in the Western Text of Acts 8:37, which reports the eunuch as replying to Philip, "I believe that Jesus Christ is the Son of God." Evidently this equation was a central confessional statement in the second century as well as in the first and is perhaps traceable to the church's profounder pondering of the implications of Jesus' role as Messiah in terms of His intimate relationship with the Father.

The Old Testament helps us appreciate the content also of this creedal response to God's action in Jesus. On the one hand we find a Davidic strain. In his message to David, Nathan repeats the words of the Lord concerning the son who is to succeed him: "He shall build a house for My name, and I will establish the throne of his kingdom forever. I will be his father, and he shall be My son" (2 Sam. 7:13-14). The passage helps sketch the pattern for the understanding of Jesus' relationship to God, for Jesus is the Son of David in a special sense of the word. Since the king in the Old Testament is associated with God in terms of a father-son relationship, we are not surprised to find in some manuscripts of Luke 3:22 the pronouncement: "Today I have begotten Thee." These words are taken from Ps. 2, which speaks of the ultimate victory of the king over his enemies. Jesus as David's greater Son is the hope of the New Israel. In similar vein Paul asserts that Jesus was "descended from David according to the flesh and designated Son of God in power." (Rom. 1:3-4)

The second strain is an identification of Jesus with Israel. Imbedded in the popular consciousness was a passage like Is. 44:1-2: "But now hear, O Jacob My servant, Israel whom I have chosen! Thus says the Lord who made you, who formed you from the womb and will help you." This picture of Israel as a collective unit is balanced by a more individualistic note expressed in Is. 42:1: "Behold My servant, whom

I uphold, My chosen, in whom My soul delights."
A strange blending of these two ideas is made in
Is. 49:3, 6. In v. 3 the servant is called Israel: "You
are my servant, Israel, in whom I will be glorified."
But in v. 6 this servant is to "raise up the tribes of
Jacob and to restore the preserved of Israel." The
language used by the voice from heaven ("Thou art
My beloved Son; with Thee I am well pleased,"
Luke 3:22) at Jesus' baptism clearly points in the
direction of these passages and especially to Is. 44:
1-2, "But now hear, O Jacob My servant, Israel whom
I have chosen! Thus says the Lord who made you,
who formed you from the womb and will help you."
A complex association of ideas is at work here. Jesus
is the consummation of Israel as God's selected people. The word "beloved" is equivalent to "selected"
or "elected" (cf. Is. 44:1-2 LXX). Israel was the elect
of God to be a light to the nations (Is. 42:6). Israel
failed in her mission. Jesus is the embodiment of
all that Israel was designed to be. He is the embodiment of Israel. In Him all the language concerning Israel's responsibilities and the Servant's role,
especially that of suffering (Is. 53), finds its proper
interpretation and commentary.

Such understanding underlies the unusual use of
Hos. 11:1 in Matt. 2:15. Hosea had written about
Israel's deliverance from Egypt: "When Israel was a
child, I loved him, and out of Egypt I called My
son." Matt. 2:15 says that the return of Jesus from
Egypt was in fulfillment of this passage. What does

he mean? He means that Jesus as the consummation of Israel recapitulates the experience of Israel. There is a continuity between God's activity in connection with Israel and with Jesus. But God's intent is one of compassion and concern for Israel, as the balance of the 11th chapter of Hosea observes. In Jesus God shows that He has mercy on His people.

The Gospels are replete with expressions of the intimate relationship Jesus enjoys with His Father. In contrast with Platonic and Stoic thought, which spoke of the fatherhood of God in terms of ultimate origins, Jesus spoke of the love and care of a heavenly Father in a context of filial devotion and obedience. God is the Father of Israel because He selected her out of all the nations of the earth to be the special instrument of His purposes. God has made all the nations, but Israel is His son in an extraordinary sense (Hos. 11:1), for Israel is the recipient of His special care and concern. What is said of Israel applies to Jesus, but in the Gospels we are confronted with the fact that Jesus understands Himself to be in a unique relationship with God. Out of that unique relationship and self-understanding stems His authoritative expression. Because He is what He is, the disciples in association with Him are brought into a fresh and vital relationship with the Father. This is the meaning of the strange passage: "I thank thee, Father, Lord of heaven and earth, that Thou hast hidden these things from the wise and understanding and revealed them to babes; yea,

Father, for such was Thy gracious will. All things have been delivered to Me by My Father; and no one knows the Son except the Father, and no one knows the Father except the Son and anyone to whom the Son chooses to reveal Him." (Matt. 11: 25-27)

While the accent in the Gospels is on the unique *relationship* of Jesus with the Father, we are never to forget the *mission* of God's Son. The account of Jesus' visit to Jerusalem at the age of 12 is thematic. Jesus asserts in His correction of Mary's statement that He must be in His Father's house (Luke 2:49): "Son, why have You treated us so? Behold, Your father and I have been looking for You anxiously" (v. 48). His sense of joint ownership with the Father is expressed in His zeal for the Lord's house when He cast out the money-changers and said, "My house shall be a house of prayer; but you have made it a den of robbers." (19:46)

Jesus' recognition of His unique assignment is signaled by the synoptists in their accent on the temptation of Jesus at the beginning of His public ministry. The temptation accounts depict the dimensions of the struggle in which Jesus is to be engaged. The question is: Will He be Messiah on God's terms or on His own terms? The proposition is subtle: "If You are the Son of God, command these stones to become loaves of bread" (Matt. 4:3). It is beside the point to suggest that Jesus' sonship is put into question through the "if" approach. On the contrary, the point is granted for the sake of argument. The temptation rather lies in this, that Satan suggests to Jesus, "You are the Son of God. Act like one. Why starve yourself when You enjoy such privilege?" In other words, "Look out for Yourself." The temptations are repeated at the crucifixion. The chief priests say, "He trusts in God; let God deliver Him now if He desires Him; for He said, 'I am the Son of God'" (Matt. 27:43). "If You are the Son of God, come down from the cross" (27:40). It seemed indeed that He was a failure. But He had earlier made His decision. His prayer in the Garden, "Father, if Thou art willing, remove this cup from Me; nevertheless not My will but Thine, be done" (Luke 22:42), clearly shows the direction of His mind.

Because Jesus is truly Israel, incorporation with Him makes possible an Israel of redeemed people. In Jesus' sonship with the Father lies the possibility of our own sonship, as the apostle Paul expresses it: "In Christ Jesus you are all sons of God through faith. For as many of you as were baptized into Christ have put on Christ" (Gal. 3:26-27). In the confession, "I believe that Jesus is the Christ, the Son of God," we find our own identity. At the same time confession of His name places us in similar jeopardy. Hence He warns us: "Whoever is ashamed of Me and of My words, of him will the Son of Man be ashamed when He comes in His glory and the glory of the Father and of the holy angels" (Luke 9:26). Peter had to learn the price.

5

Jesus Is Lord

"Who is like Thee, O Lord, among the gods?
Who is like Thee, majestic in holiness, terrible in
glorious deeds, doing wonders?" sang Moses and
Israel in Ex. 15:11. In response to Joshua's call to
serve the Lord, the people reply, "Therefore we also
will serve the Lord, for He is our God." (Josh. 24:18)

What is affirmed in these passages is that the
God of Israel is One who has made Himself the
exclusive Leader of Israel through His distinctive
character and deeds. By virtue of His overthrow of
the Egyptians God has laid claim on Israel, and the
proper response of Israel is obedience. In contrast
to the heathen, who do not know God (Ps. 79:6;
Jer. 10:25), Israel is in a personal relation with Jahweh, the Lord.

The New Testament underscores this confession.

According to Matt. 11:25 God is the Father, Lord of heaven and earth. 1 Tim. 6:15 declares that He is the "blessed and only Sovereign, the King of kings and Lord of lords." Paul at Mars' Hill confirms that God "made the world and everything in it, being Lord of heaven and earth" (Acts 17:24). In all this there is the understanding that God has special claims of ownership and lays a proper claim to devotion. In flagrant challenge, Satan claims ownership of God's people, and authority is indeed given him for a time (John 12:31; 16:11), but ultimately he faces defeat (Rev. 12:9; 20:2-3, 10). Jesus points up the issue as He asserts the sovereign rights of God in His famous rejoinder to the devil: "You shall worship the Lord your God, and Him only shall you serve." (Matt. 4:10)

Alongside this confession of God's lordship we find New Testament writers applying to Jesus what is said of God in the Old Testament. In his letter to the Romans Paul states that if one confesses with his lips that "Jesus is Lord," he "will be saved" (10:9). The formula appears to have imbedded itself early in the proclamation. "God has made Him both Lord and Christ," said Peter of Jesus (Acts 2:36). And from 1 Cor. 12:3 ("No one can say, 'Jesus is Lord,' except by the Holy Spirit"), because of its association with questions of liturgical propriety, it is possible to conclude that the formula was in use as a community creedal expression. A polemical interest is suggested by 1 Cor. 8:5-6: "For although

there may be so-called gods in heaven or on earth —
as indeed there are many 'gods' and many 'lords' —
yet for us there is one God, the Father, from whom
are all things and for whom we exist, and one Lord,
Jesus Christ, through whom are all things and
through whom we exist."

Paul's words to the Philippians (2:6-11) express
the procedure whereby Jesus arrived at the pronouncement of His Lordship:

> . . . Christ Jesus, who, though He was in the form of
> God, did not count equality with God a thing to be
> grasped but emptied Himself, taking the form of a
> servant, being born in the likeness of men. And be-
> ing found in human form He humbled Himself and
> became obedient unto death, even death on a cross.
> Therefore God has highly exalted Him and bestowed
> on Him the name which is above every name, that
> at the name of Jesus every knee should bow in
> heaven and on earth and under the earth and every
> tongue confess that Jesus Christ is Lord, to the glory
> of God the Father.

Unlike Adam, who grasped at equality with God,
Jesus was willing to let His true status be obscured
by adopting the role of a slave, the very contrary
of lordship. In his self-effacement and obedience
to the assigned task of dying like a common criminal
we see the portrait of the Suffering Servant of Is. 53.
This is His way to receipt of the name that is above
all names — Lord. Every knee should bow and every
tongue should confess that the one to be acknowledged as Lord is none other than Jesus Christ. God

claims such tribute for Himself in Is. 45:23: "By Myself I have sworn, from My mouth has gone forth in righteousness a word that shall not return: 'To Me every knee shall bow, every tongue shall swear.' " Submission and obedience. They are the marks of the confessor of the Lord God. And these are to be accorded Jesus. God is the Father who is concerned for His people. He gives the Son, and the Son carries out His task. And God appoints Him the Inheritor and the Sharer of all that properly belongs to Himself. In the exaltation of Jesus God's character finds overt expression. Hence the honor paid to Jesus spells the glory of the Father.

To confess Jesus as the Christ means that one recognizes Him as the Helper of Israel. To recognize Him as Lord means to assert that this Jesus the Christ is not simply a national hero but the Ruler of the universe who has just title to all who confess His name. He is above all lesser claimants. Hence we are to reverence Him as Lord (1 Peter 3:15). Since that understanding comes only through faith, "No one can say, 'Jesus is Lord,' except by the Holy Spirit" (1 Cor. 12:3). It is not surprising that when Paul considers the various relations of Christians he instinctively changes from the accent on Christ, for example, in Col. 3:1-16, to Lord in 3:18-24. What he is saying is this, that all status on the human level must be viewed in terms of the status we enjoy relative to Jesus Christ, who by virtue of His deed of love for us is our Lord, our Master. Similarly when Paul speaks of orders or traditions received from Jesus Christ, he speaks of "the Lord" (1 Cor. 7:12, 25, 40; 9:14; 11:23; 14:37; 1 Thess. 4:15). As the One who is the supreme Authority He is "Lord both of the dead and of the living" (Rom. 14:9). Hence He comes finally to judge all men (Acts 17:31; cf. Phil. 4:5). Just as Israel was to understand her role as one of obedience to the God who saved her, so the Christian is to see the moral and ethical implications of this recognition of Christ's claim to ownership expressed so often in such a phrase as "Paul, a slave of Christ Jesus." Out of such conviction the iron of steadfast confession was smelted. As the stones came flying at Stephen, he prayed, "*Lord* Jesus, receive my spirit." (Acts 7:59)

When Polycarp was asked, "What harm is it to call Caesar Lord and to burn the customary incense?" he replied after a moment of silence, "I cannot follow your counsel." When he had been brought to the site of execution, the official in charge pleaded with Polycarp to take note of his years and make the requested denial, the aged veteran replied "For eighty-six years He has been my Lord and has never wronged me. How, then, can I renounce my King who has saved me?" "But I have wild beasts," said the Roman officer. Polycarp replied, "We have no intention after making a change for the better to trade it for the worse." "If you disdain my animals, I can punish you with fire!" Polycarp answered, "You threaten me with the fire which burns only for the moment and then is quenched; but you are ignorant of the judgment to come and of the fire of eternal punishment reserved for the ungodly. But what is the point in this delay? Carry out your decision." Such was the certainty of the faith that caught the vision of One who had this name inscribed on His robe and thigh: "King of kings and Lord of lords." (Rev. 19:16)

Jesus Died and Rose

In his first letter to the Thessalonians Paul confesses, "We believe that Jesus died and rose again" (4:14). From the tradition described by Paul in 1 Cor. 15:3-5 ("For I delivered to you as of first importance what I also received, that Christ died for our sins in accordance with the Scriptures, that He was buried, that He was raised on the third day in accordance with the Scriptures, and that He appeared to Cephas, then to the Twelve") it is clear that a creedal formula to the effect "Jesus died and rose" played no small part in the church's liturgical or confessional expression. The words in Rom. 8:34 ("Who is to condemn? Is it Christ Jesus, who died, yes, who was raised from the dead, who is at the right hand of God, who indeed intercedes for us?") point in the same direction.

"Jesus died and rose." Both statements are significant. Good Friday is not a tragedy which was reversed by Easter. The death of Jesus is viewed by New Testament writers as an essential installment in God's redemptive plan. The two men on the road to Emmaus say, after reciting the grim facts, "But we had hoped that He was the One to redeem Israel" (Luke 24:21). In answer to their obtuseness Jesus counters: "Was it not necessary that the Christ should suffer these things and enter into His glory?" (v. 26). In other words, if Jesus is the Christ, the Messiah, it should not be surprising if He suffers. This is expected of the Christ; besides, it is the customary fate of Israel's prophets to be misunderstood and even rejected. (Acts 7)

Thus the early church, confronted with the "embarrassment" of the death of the Messiah, made capital out of it by insisting that His death was His very credential. That the baby lies in a manger is no proof that He is not the Messiah; on the contrary, the very lowliness is the identifying mark of the Christ (Luke 2:12). Simeon asserts that He is "for a sign that is spoken against" (2:34). Jerusalem was running true to form when it crucified Jesus Christ (13:33-34). The death of Jesus was a clash with the devil for large stakes. It marked the threshold of a new age. Lucan records in connection with the battle of Pharsalia that there were portents in earth and sky. It was the manner of antiquity to signal the decisive character of particular events in terms of cosmic disturbance. The darkness that settled over Palestine at the hour of Jesus' death made a profound impression on the participants in history's most dramatic moment. Matt. 27:51-53 observes that the curtain in the temple was torn in two from top to bottom, that the earth trembled, and the tombs were opened. The earthquake and the other strange events filled even a hardened Roman officer with awe, and we read, "Truly this was the Son of God!" (v. 54). The death of Jesus, far from being a disaster, was the distinctive mark of His mission, and it brought faith to birth.

The account of the opening of the tombs echoes Ezek. 37, especially vv. 12-13: "Therefore prophesy and say to them, Thus says the Lord God: Behold, I will open your graves and raise you from your graves, O My people. . . . And you shall know that I am the Lord when I open your graves and raise you from your graves, O My people." This chapter from Ezekiel also speaks of God's servant David, who shall be king over a restored Israel. What Matthew is telling us therefore is that this hour when Jesus seems to be defeated is actually His hour of victory — the new age has been ushered in through the death of Jesus.

Nor is Matthew alone in saying this. The Fourth Gospel emphasizes that the hour of Jesus' death is the hour that spells the way to glorification (John 12:23). The recipe of success is given in the grain of wheat that died in order to beget life. And Luke cites the words of Jesus: "Was it not necessary that the Christ suffer these things and enter into His glory?" (Luke 24:26)

Jesus died *and* rose. The rising from the dead is an integral part of His total action. The resurrection is not the reversal of a tragedy, it is rather the next stage in a single activity. Through death Jesus enters into that sphere of action which gives full play to His person. Through His resurrection He is recognized for what He is — the Lord of the church and the universe. It is God who raised Him (Phil. 2:9; Acts 2:24, 32) and thereby made Jesus both Lord and Christ. (Acts 2:36)

The death and resurrection of Jesus release the powers of the new age. The longer ending to Mark attests the significance of Jesus' death and resurrection: "And these signs will accompany those who believe: In My name they will cast out demons; they will speak in new tongues; they will pick up serpents, and if they drink any deadly thing, it will not hurt them; they will lay their hands on the sick, and they will recover" (16:17). In contrast with the apocalyptic hope which placed the demonstration of the powers of the new age at the end of history, the New Testament emphasizes that the new age has begun in the person of Jesus. He rises on the *third day*. The new age begins inside history. It is contemporaneous with man's normal experience. Hence the parables of expectation, of the proper use of one's resources, of preparedness, and the like.

The powers of the new age are apparent in the

receipt of the Spirit. Exalted at the right hand of God, Jesus pours out the Spirit on His disciples in accordance with the promise of the Father (Acts 2:33). What this means is that Jesus has plenipotentiary power. All the resources of deity are at His disposal. He is in charge. In order to pour out the Spirit Jesus departs from the disciples, but only to be *with them* in a more intimate fashion (John 14:18; Matt. 28:20). At the same time they are to be *with Him.* (Eph. 2:5-6; Rom. 6:8-13)

Through His Spirit the powers of the new age become alive in us. These powers are a reality for the Christian in his baptism. It is not Biblical doctrine that life begins after death or through death. The death of our bodies does not make life possible. If there is life to come, it is a continuation of a life that has already begun. This life begins at baptism, for at the cross our death took place in Christ's death (Rom. 6:1-11). At our baptism we become recipients of the life that Jesus won for us. This life means the introduction of the Holy Spirit into our lives and the experience of release from the powers of sin (Rom. 6:2-11). Eternal life is experienced now in this receipt of the powers of the new age. We do not work for eternal life — we possess the first installments of it in the groanings of the Spirit within us (Rom. 8). Hence Paul is greatly concerned about the heresy at Corinth that there is no resurrection of the dead. That would also include Jesus Christ. But if Christ has not been raised, then our faith is futile, for we are still in our sins. Paul's point is this, that the purpose of Jesus' resurrection is to link us with the powers of the new age and to release them in us. If He did not rise, the new age is impossible. (1 Cor. 15)

Thus the resurrection hope for all men is not derived first of all from the resurrection of Jesus, but belief in the resurrection of Jesus is connected with prior belief in the resurrection of all humanity. Thus Paul declared himself in favor of Pharisaic doctrine on the resurrection in his appearance before the council. (Acts 23:6)

The resurrection means the continuation of the life begun in Jesus here on earth (Rom. 5:21). But the present body must be changed in order to achieve the objectives of the new age (1 Cor. 15:45-49). If we are deceived in this, says Paul, we are of all men most miserable. He does not mean because we have renounced so much in this world but rather because we were filled with much anticipation and then find ourselves disappointed. "If the dead are not raised, 'Let us eat and drink, for tomorrow we die'" (1 Cor. 15:32). If there is no resurrection from the dead, then we are left with the hopelessness of the pagan world about us, for in that slogan much of antiquity, outside the mystery cults, expressed its bankruptcy regarding any hope after death.

The gravestones of the Mediterranean world eloquently attest the heavier stone that lay rolled over the bosom of humanity.

Chiseled on a pre-Christian monument in Rome is this series of questions:

Why dost thou rob me from my mother's knee?
O Hades, never sated, why this haste?
Breathes one who shall not pay his debt to thee?

Few pictures are more poignant than that of the grandmother who sits gracefully robed and holds a toy bird in one hand while she looks at her grandchild held tenderly on her lap with the other. The inscription reads:

This is my daughter's child I hold. We fed
In life our eyes on all the sun's bright rays.
Now dead, upon my knees I hold the dead.

Typical is this lament of an unwedded woman:

Lament, O passer-by, my short-lived hour
And stand a moment near my funeral urn.
From mourn to night for all my bitter fate
The ones who bore me shed a frequent tear —
They saw no wedding day come in its turn.
No singer played before my bridal bower.

There was, of course some whistling in the dark, but the general tone is somber and joyless. It took words like these to roll the stone away:

" 'O death, where is thy victory? O death, where is thy sting?' The sting of death is sin, and the power of sin is the Law. But thanks be to God, who gives us the victory through our Lord Jesus Christ." (1 Cor. 15:55-57)

7

Jesus Is Savior

The simple eloquence of Israel's ancient creed bears repetition:

A wandering Aramean was my father; and he went down into Egypt and sojourned there, few in number; and there he became a nation, great, mighty, and populous. And the Egyptians treated us harshly and afflicted us and laid upon us hard bondage. Then we cried to the Lord, the God of our fathers, and the Lord heard our voice and saw our affliction, our toil, and our oppression; and the Lord brought us out of Egypt with a mighty hand and an outstretched arm, with great terror, with signs and wonders; and He brought us into this place and gave us this land, a land flowing with milk and honey. And behold, now I bring the first of the fruit of the ground, which Thou, O Lord, hast given me. (Deut. 26:5-10)

These words were recited as a part of the liturgy of the firstfruits, in which the worshiper through his presentation of the earliest part of the crop acknowledged Jahweh's gift of the land of Canaan and His prior rights to all its fruits. Israel does not base her faith on mystical experience or philosophical speculation. Israel identifies herself in terms of a signal deliverance wrought by God. "I am the Lord your God, who brought you out of the land of Egypt, out of the house of bondage" (Ex. 20:2). The psalmists do not permit Israel to forget it. (Ps. 66; 103:6-7; 135; 136; 78; 106; 77)

Each generation of Israelites identified with the first participants. "A wandering Aramean was *my* father.... And the Egyptians treated *us* harshly.... Then we cried . . . the Lord heard our voice. . . ."

Out of the certainty of that deliverance evolved the certainty of deliverance in other situations, for "Israel is saved by the Lord with everlasting salvation" (Is. 45:17). God can be counted on, for He is righteous. He keeps His end of the bargain which He has made with Israel. He does not leave them at the mercy of their enemies. "There is no other god besides Me, a righteous God and a Savior; there is none besides Me" (45:21). He is the "Holy One of Israel," but instead of consuming His rebellious people in wrath, He approaches them as "Savior" and "Redeemer." (Is. 43:3, 14)

This assurance was to sustain Israel in the hours of apparent national disaster. Jahweh would pull them through. God's past record was a guarantee for the future. Hence in Is. 51:9-11 the first exodus becomes the basis for the hope of a second exodus — from the Babylonian captivity. The God who rescues Israel out of Babylon will also send deliverance at the end of days. Isaiah writes:

> How beautiful upon the mountains are the feet of him who brings good tidings, who publishes peace, who brings good tidings of good, who publishes salvation, who says to Zion, "Your God reigns." Hark, your watchmen lift up their voice, together they sing for joy; for eye to eye they see the return of the Lord to Zion. Break forth together into singing, you waste places of Jerusalem; for the Lord has comforted his people, he has redeemed Jerusalem. The Lord has bared His holy arm before the eyes of all the nations; and all the ends of the earth shall see the salvation of our God. (52:7-10)

The future is pregnant with hope. And the message of the New Testament is that in Jesus the end time has come, that He marks the completion of God's salvation effort. Another way of saying it is that He comes in the fullness of time (Gal. 4:4). Acts 4:12 disqualifies all competitors, stating that "there is no other name under heaven given among men by which we must be saved."

It does not appear, however, that the early community used the formulation "Jesus is Savior" in precisely this succinct form. The expression itself is rare in the Gospels (Luke 2:11 and John 4:42 are notable exceptions), in Acts, and in Paul. On the other hand, the mind of the early community is clearly oriented in the direction of this equation, and a number of statements suggest that the formula is implicit as a primary affirmation in the confessional utterances of the primitive community to the effect that Jesus is in continuity with all that God has been doing in the past.

Just as the exodus was the central fact in Israel's history, so Jesus marks a new exodus experience for Israel of the new covenant. Luke 9:31 records that Moses and Elijah "spoke of His departure, which He was to accomplish at Jerusalem." The word for departure here in the original is "exodus." It may well be that Luke intends a *double-entendre*. The euphemistic expression for death would remind the Christian reader of Jesus' role as a second Moses engaged in deliverance of the New Israel. In any event the accent on the Passover preparations in the synoptists with emphasis on the new covenant (Matt. 26:28) clearly indicates that Jesus is God's great salvation gift to the church and that in His person He achieves a deliverance of which the first exodus, one might say, is but a working model. The importance of the event is signaled by the tradition concerning Jesus' action and words that night. St. Paul writes:

> For I received from the Lord what I also delivered to you, that the Lord Jesus on the night when He was betrayed took bread, and when He had given thanks, He broke it and said, "This is My body which is for you. Do this in remembrance of Me." In the same way also the cup after supper, saying, "This cup is the new covenant in My blood. Do this, as often as you drink it, in remembrance of Me."

For as often as you eat this bread and drink the cup, you proclaim the Lord's death until He comes. (1 Cor. 11:23-26)

To this culminating action all Jesus' miracles point. God's salvation showed itself in His actions toward Israel. So also Jesus reveals the nature of His person in His saving acts. He heals the paralytic to underscore the forgiveness of sins which He brings (Mark 2), for He is the person who links man with God. Hence He designedly eats with publicans and sinners. He does not speak abstractly of forgiveness but pronounces absolution on Peter by taking Peter into His own salvation program (Luke 5:1-11). Moses fed multitudes in the wilderness. Jesus reveals Himself as the source of supply for Israel by feeding crowds that followed Him (John 6). He spells the end of Satan's reign, but He points dramatically to the fact by casting out demons (Luke 11:20). Each of His healings is a signpost indicating His larger task, which is to usher in the great day of the Lord's salvation. "Jesus did many other signs," says John, ". . . but these are written that you may believe that Jesus is the Christ, the Son of God, and that believing you may have life in His name" (John 20:30-31). All His activity, all His living, all His suffering, all His dying — all is the expression of God's culminating salvation. Christianity is not good views but good news. It is not philosophical propositions or mystical absorption. It is the message of God's deed of love expressed in a person.

The salvation is clearly God's. Israel did not merit salvation. Justification by grace is not a Pauline discovery. Paul knew well what Deut. 9:4-5 said:

> Do not say in your heart, after the Lord your God has thrust them out before you, "It is because of my righteousness that the Lord has brought me in to possess this land"; whereas it is because of the wickedness of these nations that the Lord is driving them out before you. Not because of your righteousness or the uprightness of your heart are you going in to possess their land; but because of the wickedness of these nations the Lord your God is driving them out from before you, and that He may confirm the word which the Lord swore to your fathers, to Abraham, to Isaac, and to Jacob.

The best commentary on Paul's doctrine of salvation and the role played by the Spirit is to be had in Ezek. 36:22-32:

> Therefore say to the house of Israel, Thus says the Lord God: It is not for your sake, O house of Israel, that I am about to act, but for the sake of My holy name, which you have profaned among the nations to which you came. And I will vindicate the holiness of My great name, which has been profaned among the nations and which you have profaned among them; and the nations will know that I am the Lord, says the Lord God, when through you I vindicate My holiness before their eyes. For I will take you from the nations and gather you from all the countries and bring you into your own land. I will sprinkle clean water upon you, and you shall be clean from all your uncleannesses, and from all your idols I will cleanse you. A new heart I will give you, and a new spirit I will put within you; and I will

take out of your flesh the heart of stone and give you a heart of flesh. And I will put My Spirit within you and cause you to walk in My statutes and be careful to observe My ordinances. You shall dwell in the land which I gave to your fathers; and you shall be My people, and I will be your God. And I will deliver you from all your uncleannesses; and I will summon the grain and make it abundant and lay no famine upon you. I will make the fruit of the tree and the increase of the field abundant that you may never again suffer the disgrace of famine among the nations. Then you will remember your evil ways and your deeds that were not good; and you will loathe yourselves for your iniquities and your abominable deeds. It is not for your sake that I will act, says the Lord God; let that be known to you. Be ashamed and confounded for your ways, O house of Israel.

And what clearer exposition of Paul's phrase about justifying the ungodly (Rom. 5:6) than this word from Is. 43:22-25?

Yet you did not call upon Me, O Jacob; but you have been weary of Me, O Israel! You have not brought Me your sheep for burnt offerings or honored Me with your sacrifices. I have not burdened you with offerings or wearied you with frankincense. You have not bought Me sweet cane with money or satisfied Me with the fat of your sacrifices. But you have burdened Me with your sins, you have wearied Me with your iniquities. I, I am He who blots out your transgressions for My own sake, and I will not remember your sins.

Just as the Old Testament accents the initiative

of God — God is Savior (Is. 43:11) — so the New Testament emphasizes that it is God who gives Jesus voluntarily. God loves the world and gives His only Son (John 3:16). God is not reconciled by men. On the contrary, God reconciles men to Himself. "All this is from God, who through Christ reconciled us to Himself and gave us the ministry of reconciliation." (2 Cor. 5:18)

But just as Israel looked forward to an ultimate consummation, so the church, in continuity with Israel, looks forward to the fuller realization of the meaning of redemption. This is the paradox — we are saved and yet not saved. The misunderstanding of this paradox has cost the church much in misspent dogmatic argument. On the one hand, Paul observes in Rom. 8:24 that "we were saved," and in 5:1 he concludes, "Therefore, since we are justified by faith, we have peace with God through our Lord Jesus Christ." This is the theological indicative present. On the other hand in 13:11 the apostle says that "salvation is nearer to us now than when we first believed." And in 5:9 the paradox is explicitly expressed: "Since, therefore, we are now justified by His blood, much more shall we be saved by Him from the wrath of God." 1 Peter 1:5 leans in the same direction with its words about those "who by God's power are guarded through faith for a salvation ready to be revealed in the last time." Again Heb. 9:28 observes that "Christ, having been offered once to bear the sins of many, will appear a second time, not to deal with sin but to save those who are eagerly waiting for Him."

The key to all this is given in Phil. 3:20-21. Paul writes:

> But our commonwealth is in heaven, and from it we await a Savior, the Lord Jesus Christ, who will change our lowly body to be like His glorious body, by the power which enables Him even to subject all things to Himself.

The powers of the new age are not capable of being realized fully in the present order of things. Just as Israel of old looked for a new heaven and a new earth (Is. 65:17), so God's Israel now looks for the consummation of all things. "According to His promise we wait for new heavens and a new earth in which righteousness dwells" (2 Peter 3:13). Or as the apostle Paul expresses it: "We know that the whole creation has been groaning in travail together until now; and not only the creation but we ourselves, who have the firstfruits of the Spirit, groan inwardly as we wait for adoption as sons, the redemption of our bodies." (Rom. 8:22-23)

The purpose of salvation is that we might enjoy the gifts of the Spirit. Some of these are enumerated in Gal. 5:22-23: "But the fruit of the Spirit is love, joy, peace, patience, kindness, goodness, faithfulness, gentleness, self-control." These are, however, but an installment, as Paul observes in Rom. 8:23, of grander things to come. In the meantime we have the flesh, the old nature, the self-in-rebellion-against-

God, which is always attempting to claim us under the Law (Gal. 5:18-21). The prospect of the larger hope prompts Paul to exclaim: "My desire is to depart and be with Christ, for that is far better." (Phil. 1:23)

Thus salvation is always a present reality, only we move on various plateaus — and the highest is reserved for us at the end of the end time. It is like climbing a mountain. At every bend in the trail there are fresh wonders, but the vista at the top — that is what travelers who have been there say we must see.

The salvation to come is not limited to human beings. The Biblical view is cosmic. Col. 1:20 declares that through Jesus Christ God aims to "reconcile to Himself all things, whether on earth or in heaven, making peace by the blood of His cross." "The creation itself will be set free from its bondage to decay and obtain the glorious liberty of the children of God." (Rom. 8:21)

Selected Bibliography

Cullmann, Oscar. *The Earliest Christian Confessions*. Trans. J. K. S. Reid. London: Lutterworth Press, 1949.

Dodd, Charles Harold. *The Apostolic Preaching and Its Developments*. London: Hodder & Stoughton Limited, 1936 (New edition reset 1944 & seventh impression 1951).

Kelly, John N. D. *Early Christian Creeds*. London: Longmans (first published 1950, second edition 1960).

Neufeld, Vernon H. *The Earliest Christian Confessions*. ("New Testament Tools and Studies," V). Grand Rapids: Wm. B. Eerdmans, 1963. Detailed bibliography, pp. 147–54.

Stauffer, Ethelbert. *New Testament Theology*. Trans. from the German by John Marsh. New York: The Macmillan Company (trans. from the fifth German edition — first pub. in Eng. 1955, first American ed. 1956). See pp. 235–54.